THE MAGIC

OF

LEMURIA

A Journey to the Energy Sites on the Central Coast of California

Christine Auriela Aloisio

The Magic of Lemuria
A Journey to the Energy Sites
on the Central Coast of California.
By Christine Auriela Aloisio Copyright © 2015
ISBN: 978-1-4951-3943-7

Cover design by the Francis Aloisio & Lighthouse Print-USA.
Cover photo of the Pacific Valley site.
Interior design and formatting by Francis Aloisio.
1st Edition (2014): Printing by Booklocker-USA
2nd Edition (2016): Printing by Progress Press Co. Ltd. (Malta).
3rd Edition (2018): Printing by Progress Press Co. Ltd. (Malta).

The Temple Symbols and Insights by the Author.
All photos/drawings are the artwork of Francis X. Aloisio.
Map from California Division of Tourism.

Dedicated

to the

Lemurian Legacy of Love

Thank you
for Living from
the heart.
Christine♡

Acknowledgments

I would like to give acknowledgement to the published works of various authors and for their insights:

Aureiia Louise Jones: *Telos*

Barbara Hand Clow: *The Pleiadian Agenda – A New Cosmology for the Age of Light.*

Francis Xavier Aloisio: *Islands of Dream* and *The Age of Magic and Wisdom.*

Julian Websdale: *Waking Times-Sacred Sites and Energy Fields.*

Lauren O. Thyme: *The Lemurian Way.*

L Carroll & J Tober: *Kryon: The Lemurian Connection.*

Lyssa Royal: *Lemuria-A Reflection.*

Maia Kyi'Ra Nartoomid: *Thoth on the origin of Humanity.*

Mark L. & E. Clare Prophet: *The Masters and their Retreats.*

Jill Mattson: Writer, Musical & Energetic Healing Facilitator.

And my very special thanks to: my wonderful husband, Francis, who has helped me bring these writings into form through his love and support in publishing my first book.

Thanks to: The High Priest of Telos, Adama, for his insights, encouragement and love; Pati Appel: for her special friendship, support, love and timely promptings.

And to myself: for the work and love I have put into this book. I did the final editing so any errors that may appear in this publication are solely mine.

Dear Reader,

Because I want your experience to have that 'Lemurian Flow' to it, please enjoy the surprises included in this book. I will take you through my **Introduction** to tell you a bit about myself and why I put to pen this information. From there you will be lead through the **Lemurian Gateways** of the Central Coast of California and what they mean, then on to what **Lemuria** was all about and where it is today.

Along the way you will be receiving **Extra Insights** to support you on your journey to your true self, as well as your adventure through these amazing Temples/Energy Vortexes.

Of course, I will give you a **Visiting Protocol** and **Meditation** to prepare you as you get ready to head out to these sites, either physically or through visual meditation. Along with each Temple/Vortex, you will be given their **physical location and specific purpose** and vibration of each one, with the explanation in quotes from Adama.

The list of Temples is as follows: Illumination / Cayucos, Inner Knowing / Cambria, The Bridge / Moonstone Beach, Cambria, Divine Union / North Coast, Cambria, Healing Temple / San Simeon, Wisdom / Piedras Blancas, Venus / North Piedras Blancas, Peace / South Big Sur, Abundance / Pacific Valley, Big Sur.

In the back of the book, you will find some **Further Insights from Adama** as well as the **Glossary, and** an **Appendix** which includes information about the **Sacred Symbols**, **Vortexes** and **Missions of California**, the **Chumash Nation** and about the **Ten Dimensions**.

There is a small map of the sites for your perusal, and how to obtain the **Sacred Symbol Cards** through my or Francis' website. I end it all with a **small bio** about me, in case you may be interested!

Turn the page and let's get started! Shall we?

Enjoy
Your Journey
Through the Temple Sites!

Introduction

When you pick up this book, you have come to realize within yourself that Lemuria does, indeed, exist both internally within our *DNA* and outwardly, in areas around the Blue Pacific.

Welcome back to YOU! You were never lost! You just forgot. I, myself, had finally come to this conclusion and started connecting to this wondrous Lemurian Era after I found myself in the middle of Atlantis, Malta in particular.

What in the world was I doing in Atlantis?

In my karmic past I must have started out there in some way. But wait, didn't I start out in Lemuria, where most of us have? It was the wrong way round, I thought, until I decided I needed to jar some memories loose and see what came of it all. I will share my Malta experiences, later...now read on!

I do love living in the Lemurian part of the world, California that is. I love the feeling of the connectedness to nature and to those who are my Spirit family here, even traveling as often as I did to Hawaii and still love to do. It was there, in Hawaii, where I spent my last lifetime among the Alii (Royalty). I love the feeling of the softness of the energies in both California and Hawaii. It is a feminine energy that I feel compatible with, as many of you do who have a great understanding of this vibration.

So, at one point in my life, I decided to actually move back to Hawaii, where I felt most at home, due to my past life there. It is still part of who I am.

I would arrive on the islands and completely immerse myself in the language, the land and *hula,* and of course the Heiau's - ancient temples. Many times, I even have had Hawaiian natives recognize me as someone they know or knew in another life. I am aware of the location of sacred places without any guidance and I can remember the ancient chants by heart.

But I reincarnated in California, and that is where my work started in this lifetime. I grew up in Southern California and moved to the Central Coast that place in the middle of the California coast from south of San Luis Obispo up to and including Big Sur.

It is in Cambria, right in the center of this Central Coast that I finally landed with my family. I went through many transitions while living here. I had to find out who I truly am and live that truth. I found my spiritual path here. *Why?*

I believe it is because these Lemurian Temples (vortexes) that are located along the coast line (some inland and some in the sea) have influenced me and guided me along on this amazing spiritual path. I came to discover each of them on my journey. *Wow...awesomely cool!* (California speak!)

So getting back to Atlantis...I had to inevitably do some reconnecting there first to actually clear many lifetimes of anguish that started there. *Lifetimes? Anguish?* Why in the world would I want to do all that when I could go back 'home' to Hawaii and Languish, (with the Capital 'L' in front of anguish), in the good-vibes and Sweet Vibrations of Aloha? (California has *Good Vibrations*, thanks to the Beach

2

Boys and Hawaii-the Sweet Vibrations of *Aloha Oe*...thanks to Queen Liliokalni!)

I actually visualized myself with a cool tropical drink sitting on the beach and just relaxing and swimming with the dolphins, day in and day out. What a life, indeed!

But, I found myself on the Island of Malta in the midst of the summer heat and the chaos and the buildings and the ancient Atlantean temples and the Masculine power! *Wait. What?* The Feminine power was also present, but had been hidden, trapped and subjugated under eons of Masculine oppression.

Malta is an incredible place with prehistoric temples and even more ancient Atlantean energy, which, by the way, still vibrate with Feminine Goddess vibrations! I was lured there by the need to visit the Temple of Ggantija on the sister island of Gozo. (Malta is an archipelago of 3 islands: Malta, Gozo and Comino, situated in the middle of the Mediterranean Sea just below Sicily).

Oh, gee thanks! I was really excited to go! I knew I had a past life there in that Goddess Temple after Atlantis, and also during the Atlantean Era. *I just had* to go! *Go, go, got to go to Gozo!*

Oh, I found such a connection there...tears welled up each time I entered Ggantija Temple...and the other Temple, Mnajdra on the main island of Malta.

Yes! So many energetic connections there! So, Malta is also where I met my husband, Francis. We felt such a strong bond...lifetimes and lifetimes, and many lifetimes worth; all the way back to a planet out there somewhere in this or another Universe. Whew!

What were we to do, but come together? We knew this deep in our hearts and we also knew that it might be a seemingly very hard task, as he is *very* Atlantean and I am *very* Lemurian. Two very different ideologies and energies!

How in the world would these two people come together and why? We ask ourselves this every day! Yet we truly appreciate why we met, through our karmic and soul agreements that we made to each other. And it is the love from thousands of lifetimes that we have between us that moves all of this. We both have a wonderful way of understanding the other that overrides any of our cultural, physical and some of those natural emotional differences. Our spirits and souls are so connected and vibrate at a very high level with one another. This, plus the fact we know that we have agreed to come again in this lifetime to help in the evolution of each other and the world.

What a task! What were we thinking? Are you thinking the same? Are you doing the same?

We, like many others, are here to rebalance the energies of Atlantis and Lemuria as Divine Masculine/Feminine, Yin/Yang, Solar/Lunar, Mind/Heart. We represent these vibrations and, again like so many of us, have chosen to play this role and bring it to the world as such. Holy Moly! Big bites to chew!

Well, I have to say, we are having fun doing all this, and we decided to just enjoy it. Easier said...she pointed out with

4

a knowing grin. "What Fun we all do for the Kingdom." Right? (Francis speak!).

So, yes, I found out (am still finding out) about the truth of who I am by making these choices and by traveling to many historic and energetic sacred sites around the world, most particularly the vibrational center of Atlantis on Malta. But I will let you find out more about that amazing place through Francis' books: *Islands of Dream, The Age of Magic and Wisdom, The New Temple Dreamers* and *An Alternative Handbook to the Maltese Temples.* He helps bring into perspective the reasons for the ancient Temples and how Malta was this energetic center during all the different periods within the Atlantean Era.

Back to Lemuria; well, let me see...I can tell you that through all my experiences in Atlantis, I found that I have come even more into the understanding that Lemuria is in my ancestry, just as it is in many of yours, even if you currently feel more linked to Atlantis. Surprised? Well, that's OK, you can be, but now it is time to claim this Lemurian ancestry.

I know, I know this seems hard, since Lemuria was mostly etheric and Atlantis, well...let me tell you, those guys knew how to be in third dimension. They used gravity to the utmost and built temples to help assist in this task as well as connect back to our star ancestors and family. Lemurians liked to live in their heart center and stayed connected to the Creator and to Source and only touched a bit onto this

5

Earthly, gravity filled dimension. Interesting...yes? Yes! We loved staying in 'La La Land', so to speak.

The 'Temples' that they/we Lemurians created are all etheric, so one must be attuned to their vibrations to re-unite with their frequencies. All these energies were left in the stones around these vortexes and still vibrate there to this day.

OK then! As you can imagine, my journey brought me to Mount Shasta in Northern California and the wonders of the Lemurian Crystal City of Telos that exists in the Fifth Dimension under that majestic mountain (as well as the whole state of California). I did this with the guidance of Adama, the High Priest of that most energetic and etheric place.

My experience with this 'way cool' guy has made quite an impact on my life. In fact, he is always given me a gentle push even in writing this book.

As I traveled, many times alone, to this incredibly highly vibrational place called Shasta, I became more and more aware of what we, as Lemurians, went through during this Era in the Earth's energetic field. I was led to many sacred places on this mountain, and really became enveloped in the frequencies of Lemuria and Telos. *What? Enveloped?* So I was snugged in real cozy inside the envelope with all those Lemurian guys that wanted to lead me and I had a blast.

Back to the rest of us: So we, as Lemurians, left a legacy for ourselves to help guide and support us when dealing with all the tough imbalances we would be facing. They/we did this as they journeyed through their own devolution and knew that at another future time, we as them would be going through our own evolution into the next dimension. We knew that at some future time, we would need help reconnecting back to Source. Through this reconnection, we would find our true powerful selves once again.

So as I myself, went through and am now going through all of my transitions and transmutations during my own growth and on my own spiritual path, I realized that I needed, and still do need a push, a shove, a hand, and some guidance. I found these vortexes with the support of my guides and I also received the sacred geometry (they've have turned into some great meditation symbols) that assists in the integration of the energies of these Temples.

I do trust that you will find out for yourself how these amazing vibrational vortexes, these Lemurian Temples along the coast of Central California will support you on your own evolutionary journey.

As my dear friend, Lisa, would say: "Happy Trails!"

****

Extra Insights:

The presentation offered here comes from many different places: from delving into many different areas of informative sources, from intuitive perception and inspirations, from my own personal inner knowingness, from the insights of other worldly guides and beings, and from connecting my mind and heart to receive them through my Higher Self.

****

To give a bit of informative background about we Lemurians here is a great explanation:

"The human development and evolution of consciousness on Earth took place in **'four stages.'**

"The **first stage** was during the time of Lemuria, a civilization that was spread all over the Pacific area. It was the Lemurians who first brought forth a new race of Enlightened Beings on the planet, giving birth to *homo sapiens sapiens* – the modern human. They developed the 'intuitive mind' and ushered the separation of the 'genders.'

"The **second stage** of human spiritual evolution took place during the era of Atlantis. The Atlanteans wanted to be more grounded and less etheric; they had an impulse to descend into matter and build a more physical creation on Earth. Most importantly, they were entrusted to develop the Concrete Mind, the development of individuality and the evolution of the Human Ego."

(*Read the* novel: ***The Age of Magic and Wisdom*** by F. X. Aloisio *for more information about the 3rd and 4th Stages of the Human Evolution of Consciousness*).

Lemurian Gateways on Central Coast

Welcome to the Central Coast of California and the magical energy that lives here! California is one of many very special places in the Pacific arena that carry the ancient vibrations of Lemuria. What was/is Lemuria?

It was the Golden Era, when our Star Being family came to Gaia for the first time. They were solely connected with the Creator Source and wanted to feel the energies of Earth's special magnetic forces. Many say it was the Pleiadians who first landed here in their etheric dimension and started to 'play' with the vibrations here on this third planet from the Galactic Sun. Others say it was also the Sirians, as well as many other star beings that land here on Earth. Nonetheless, these beings, our ancestors, were very loving and had a desire for peace and knowledge.

As a result, the people of Lemuria never had religion. It was an ideology that was part of the control that happened after the end of their time. So they honored everyone's spiritual truth and knew it was unique to each individual. The one common denominator was their belief in love, compassion, joy and respect for each other and that of the Earth, as well as a higher power that resides in each *sentient* being. These traits held the basis, or the very foundation of belief in the spirit or in spirituality. So, during these times, no matter what you 'claim your religion to be,' as long as these basic truths were present, and there was honor for one another's beliefs, then each knew they are one in spirit.

9

So, to put a long story short, the Era of these 'Earth Beings' covered thousands and thousands of years on our planet and they were inhabitants of the Land of 'Mu' - the Lemurian continent, that extended from the west side of North and South America over what is now the Pacific Ocean to Australia, New Zealand, and up to the East part of Asia. Most of the islands in the Pacific are the mountaintops of this continent, many being volcanic. They were all part of the Land of 'Mu,' this amazingly large continent named for a star in the constellation of the Pleiades. We are the descendants of these peace-loving beings, and it is now time to remember that.

In fact, these beings are known to be our distant ancient ancestors, not only of ourselves, but of many indigenous tribes who are still holding this Sacred Knowledge. These tribes are in many parts of the Pacific World, like the tribes of the Aborigines of Australia who are still very closely related to the Lemurians, as well as the Native Americans.

After the great floods of this Era, many Lemurians retreated to Earth's inner kingdom, known as *Agartha*. Some were daring enough to stay on the surface and knew that they had 'work' to do in the third dimensional realm. The rest retreated and have remained in the crystal cities underground.

Those still on the surface knew they were devolving slowly into the heavier density of the Earth's vibrational field. During this time, they had to find ways to reconnect back to their true beingness, as they were losing their abilities during the shift that was occurring.

"So they prepared themselves for several thousand years to be the sacred keepers of the records of the Earth. They knew it was very important that the information they held be saved for when the waters receded, otherwise, the entire history of the Earth and the sacred teachings of the Lemurian (civilization) would have been lost." (*Lemuria - A Reflection* - Germane through Lyssa Royal).

****

Extra Insights: There is another world beneath the surface of the Earth (or Gaia) called Agartha. The many cities and places under our feet, in the Inner Earth, mostly exist in fifth dimension.

Many inhabitants of Lemuria fled to these subterranean areas under Mount Shasta during the end times of the Lemurian Era, and are represented and lead by their high priest, Adama. They have evolved into fifth dimensional beings during the many thousands of years of their existence there. The crystal city that many presently abide in is under Mount Shasta and is known as 'Telos'.

Currently, the area under the whole state of California is now called the *UnderLand of Telos/Lemuria*. The openings, in and around Mount Shasta, serve as portals to the expanded city, which has now extended itself outwardly. Consequently, there are many entrances and openings under

11

water off the California coast that are part of the network of the 'UnderLand of Telos.'

Just as the Lemurians built their crystal city of Telos, so have the Atlanteans. Mandura, the High Priest of this incredible realm, revealed the existence of their Crystal City of 'Ashua.ra.ta.ra'. These people of Atlantis too, started out in third and fourth dimension and have evolved through the millennia into fifth dimensional beings. They escaped the great floods as well, during their own Atlantean Era. Their Crystal city exists under most of Malta and the extending area of the Mediterranean to become also, the 'UnderLand of Ashua.ra.ta.ra/Atlantis.' Mandura describes perfectly the Agartha network: "Crystal Cities are a reminder of times past and futures to come."

(Check out my second book: *The Crystal City of Atlantis,* where we journey to this highly vibrational place under the sacred islands of Malta!)

****

Lemuria Today

As you know, California has always been known as a place calling many souls from all over the world to enjoy an ever-growing climate of alternative belief systems, ways of thinking, understanding, creativity and expression.

Many have also flocked to the Mountain of Shasta with its majestic and magnetizing energies to connect with Lemuria and more specifically, Telos.

As previously noted, Telos is a most special fifth dimensional crystal city, located under Mount Shasta. It is the current residing place of the Lemurians who made their home under the surface of the Earth during the cataclysm that happened during the end of their Era.

Many years before this event, they began preparing themselves by going underground. Here they learned how to live and use this environment to sustain their people. These sacred beings built a strong network of loving communities. Then, as the time came to be permanently underground, at the time of the floods, they went to work to preserve the knowledge of the Earth.

These beings are quite happy to stay in their world of peace and joy and love, and have chosen to live in their underground world away from the conflict on the surface.

These Inner Earth people, part of the Agartha network, have evolved quite rapidly during many generations and have built their etheric crystal cities that are totally independent from ours. They have raised their vibrations to a fifth dimensional reality and can live hundreds of our Earth years. Those who live longest have the strongest link to our extraterrestrial family. Many of the legends and stories of this time are in hidden stories of many religious texts all over the globe.

But, Mount Shasta cannot be the only place that still holds the vibrations of Lemuria, since it existed in so many places! Everyone knows of Hawaii, Tahiti, Australia, the Easter Islands, Japan, as well as Peru and so many places that hold this power as well. The California Coast still vibrates with many energetic vortexes that resonate with its Lemurian past, due also to the expansion of the 'UnderLand of Telos.' These vortexes are still vibrating, yet they have stayed in dormancy...until now!

****

What are these Temples and why are they here?

These Temples are gateways, back to the time when our ancestors (or us) were finding that they needed help and support as they felt their energies devolving into the gravity field of Earth. It was during the last millennia of their existence, that they (or we) were losing connection with their true selves and the Creator Source.

We found we needed help to heal, recharge, reconnect and remember who we truly are - a powerful, loving being which is part of that Creator Source.

The Lemurians infused their vibrations into the stone at significant sites here on the Central Coast of California.

These sites or vortexes still hold the instilled frequencies and we have come back now to use their particular energetic vibrations in our own evolution. And, as we visit these sites, the Temples open and resonate with their original intended frequencies.

Also, as stated before, the Native Peoples of the Pacific Rim, which include Native Americans, some of China, tribes of Japan, Hawaiians and down to the Australian Aborigines, still preserve this sacred knowledge and wisdom of the Lemurians.

The elders during the Lemurian Era knew that when the new period emerged, humankind would forget and disavow the sacred teachings. So it would be a very long time before these teachings would come back after a long period of the 'Great Forgetting' as foretold by the Aboriginal elders. These teachings would subsequently emerge in every individual being, at the level that they could accept them. This is a spiritual quest for each human being, knowingly or unknowingly.

****

During the end-times of Lemuria, sacred places were created that were electro-magnetically charged, and imprinted with the Lemurian's own frequencies. Also at this time, the Whales and Dolphins were sent from Sirius to hold the wisdom of this era and of Mother Earth.

They left us a legacy where we could re-connect to these gateways, as we ourselves evolve into fifth dimension. These Temple sites are now assisting us to recharge, revitalize and re-energize all parts of our being, and they support us as we raise our own vibrations.

That is why so many of us are drawn to sacred places, such as the ones located on the Central Coast of California. These places magnetically influence and pull us here and the synchronicity of events surrounding our energy field puts us right in these energy vortexes at the perfect time. Now, as you travel to these sacred places and are present while you connect with them, you will get back in touch with Mother Earth, which in turn, awakens the spirit within you. This is what true spirituality is all about.

This Sacred Ancient Knowledge is welling up in all of us and we look for places and events to activate this 'knowingness' and to guide us once more. These memories that come to the surface in each one of us will arrive in the form of a spiritual yearning or an inner wisdom, calling us to move forward as we stay grounded.

The power of the path you take is not to be underestimated. We awaken to this power, this wisdom that has been lying dormant, with every step we take. Remember the reason why you are attracted to this book and information, and to the Lemurian Temples of the Central Coast of California, and for all sacred sites for that matter. It is because you resonate with Lemuria. It is because *You* were an ancient Lemurian. You are awakening this within yourself, and in doing so you are awakening others on this path. Honor and trust this.

16

And, please remember that with all the work that you and your spirit family do, there will not be another time of destruction, as in our past. We have learned and have come back to move ourselves and the Earth into a New Golden Era, a New and Balanced Age. So the change happens first *within* your being, not without. As you consciously accept the truth of *who you are*, you transform and transmute the energy within you. This, in turn, shifts that of the Earth and those that reside on her and around you.

Even though Mother Earth has moved herself into a fifth dimensional frequency already, we can bring our vibration up to join hers in this dance of evolution.

If you have come this far, you are brave enough to explore the unknown and this will have a deep and profound effect upon your being and every living being on Earth...just like a ripple in a pond.

****

Extra Insights: Many are waking up to the frequency that Mother Earth is sending out as she is now in the vibration of Fifth Dimension. Those who are on her frequency and dwell in this energy of Fifth Dimension are building a new foundation for humankind. And then there are those who remain in Third Dimension that reside on the Earth that still vibrates at this level. It is a concept that many are having a hard time to grasp: Earth being in two vibrations at once. Let's just say that those who are deeply entrenched in the more dense frequencies will move at their own pace, however slowly or quickly to evolve.

Those who are linking up to and vibrating to the 5th Dimension and the higher frequencies are more able to communicate and receive information with other Fifth Dimensional beings of Inner Earth, Outer Space and the higher dimensions where the rest of our Spirit Family reside.

Many of us are now living in this higher plane of existence and sometimes find that our physical bodies are going through immense 'growing pains' in many different forms. We must all find ways to help ourselves during this time of evolvement, through a variety of healing techniques. Self-healing through intention is one method that brings our vibrations in alignment with the new Cosmic Energies coming in.

****

Some ways of remembering our Power to heal our Mental, Spiritual, Emotional and Physical bodies are:

*Always Live from the Heart. The heart is more Powerful than your mind and is constantly connected to the Source, more than any other part of you. So always open up to your heart frequency and follow it.

*Everything that is visible or invisible to our physical eyes is all energy and is in a constant state of vibration; and that vibration can be shifted by YOU.

*Even though we are in a constant state of change and always influenced by Universal Cosmic vibrations, we are Powerful enough to alter ourselves within this energy.

*Experiencing the different frequencies of vibrations brings us into the higher octaves of the higher dimensions.

*And as you attune yourself to these higher octaves, you can attain very powerful healing energies that expand, nourish and purify your bodies.

*Due to the closeness of every dimension, energy is known to flow easily through each, so you may always access your future-self to obtain information for your healing.

*Also, due to this energy flow and closeness of dimensions, you may also send healing blessings to your past and future selves, as well as your Now-Self that will benefit your whole being.

*We always have access to, and may use the healing energies that Mother Nature offers us through her realm as well as the stars and planets, just as our Lemurian ancestors and elders did.

*The octaves and frequencies of sound and music highly influence our energetic field. In order to renew yourself and keep your vibrational aura healthy and vibrant, use sound and music that are on a pure level of compatibility to your heart and body's frequency.

*Select the correct frequencies that nourish your energetic field, i.e. beauty of sight, smells, sounds and nourishing, highly vibrational foods (avoiding incongruent noise, TV influences and poor food choices).

*Be aware of the energies of those around you. Choose to be in the higher vibrations of those whose frequencies match yours, or are on an elevated level. This will support you to maintain or raise your own vibration.

*Always emanate the higher frequencies of your aura consciously, so you may be a constant source of illumination and therefore are constantly protected. As your light shines, others will be affected as their energetic field shifts and their lower energies will not have any effect on yours.

****

Visiting the Temples Energy Sites
As you step into the energy of each Temple, whether physically or energetically, keep your heart open to receive and accept new ideas and let go of the past and the old.

They no longer serve you. As you do this, you will find that you accelerate even further on your path. Allow this to happen and you will better be able to connect to these Sacred Places. Keep yourself fully grounded with these energies all around you. Feel Gaia firmly supporting you. Allow yourself to be one with *Her* and draw strength from the Earth, just as your Lemurian family did, just as the local Native Americans did. (Those tribes, in particular, that lived in this area of the Central Coast of California were known as the Chumash and the Salinians).

All of these native tribes were considered wisdom-keepers, and after the floods they kept themselves separate and did not integrate with those hungry for power. As the others struggled for control, they did their best to hold on to and keep the knowledge of their ancestors. This single act would preserve this sacred consciousness for generations to come. And now the cycle is moving into the Age of Remembering as we are called to bring back the spiritual knowledge that is rooted deep within. As more and more of us take up our heart connection and the memories start coming back, those in power will have to change and shift their energy. It is now time to heal, balance and light up the world with our gifts.

Be still and sense the energy of the Earth; allow yourself to merge with the environment as our ancient ancestors did. Celebrate it, dance with it, and feel yourself bringing up the Sacred Ancient Knowledge preserved here. Keep in mind that this energy has been programmed into the rock and it is time for this information and wisdom to be released and received and honored, then you may also remember. Remember who you truly are!

So, there is no need to look for actual physical Temples, as they have merged etherically with the rock and stone. These energetic vortexes are still active, they have just been dormant, waiting for activation from the awakened ones, and yet they are still immense Energetic sites and Temples. Again, remember, that the Lemurians did not build physical Temples. They held their energies within highly charged places on Mother Earth or Gaia.

You can access these highly charged Temples by physically visiting them, or on the inner planes, by moving into a dream state or through meditation. (The Sacred Geometry of each vortex/temple increases the effectiveness of the meditative state. – *See how to access the Sacred Symbols cards on my website*). There are many temples here on Earth that are inter-dimensional, and these Lemurian vortexes are just as powerful when we connect to them and reboot them, as they help to recharge us.

All of those who have felt a significant link to Lemuria will be drawn to these Temples and will be led to them in all the ways that the spirit proceeds into their lives. And many will have already connected to them in their meditations or on the inner planes of dreams, so the Temples will feel very familiar. At the same time, as you get acquainted with these sites, also re-connect to your Star family. They too, want to join you as you remember who you are. These are your ancient relations that are also part of your Lemurian heritage.

These temples will feel your presence and open up to you. They will shift your awareness and help you to move into a Sacred Space of Divine Power, Divine Wisdom and Divine Love. They will then become more powerful for others, so those visiting these energetic gateways may too partake in the beauty, power, love and wisdom that are offered and illuminate from each Temple.

We all chose to be the pioneers of this Golden Era and our work leads the way for the awakening of all of us who call this Earth our home.

****

Getting Ready

We will now take you on a journey of the known Lemurian Gateways or Temples that are part of the Central Coast of California. Are there more of these sacred sites up and down the west coast? Of course there are!

And yet, these are the known ones that many have visited to refresh themselves and to connect, once again, to the healing of their hearts and to rebalance themselves. During our own present times, these energies are especially needed as we step into the next period of our evolution.

Now, before we begin we would like to bring in the insights of **Adama,** The High Priest of Telos, who will introduce you to these gateways:

*"**Dear Ones,** The temples you have found in your area are ones that were used most often by our Lemurian People for healing, rejuvenation, learning and connection to the heart. We lived in a world of bliss, a 'balanced bliss.' We learned many ways to heal energetically, to stay attuned to the center of the balanced state.*

As you visit each temple, stop and feel the energies of our special place. The stones and formations, even the water that surrounds each one still vibrates to the frequency of that unique temple. If you would connect with your heart and breathe, and allow the visual of what was intended at each locale, at each temple; then, you become attuned to its frequency. It would be good to bring crystals that are ready for this attunement. In that way, when you return to your home/land, you will bring the energy of that particular temple with you.

You may visit alone; yet when in a group, the vibrations are higher and the love felt is more expansive. Remember that all of our temples were built on the vibration of Love. Thusly, we attune to the higher level of consciousness that can vibrate to this frequency. When crystals are brought to each temple, they attune to this frequency as your own little 'temples.' Then they may be brought anywhere and used to balance and influence the vibration there. You know Love travels faster than any other frequency.

Select your crystals wisely as they have important jobs to do. As you do, these crystals also will choose who they want to be with and where they want to go. We will now go through each temple as you visit them and give insights on each one. The temples will be opened and then ready for visitors. This is an exciting project! And I am extremely happy it is now here in your awareness.

Your Loving Brother, Adama."

(Please note that with each temple, I, Adama, will give you the insights for that energetic gateway).

****

Come with us now, as we take you to each of the Gateways or Temples and you step back into the Truth of Who *You* are.

As stated before, **The Coastal Temples are situated on some major pathways of highly charged Electromagnetic Energy or Ley-lines**. Be as conscious as you can when coming into these sacred energy points to clear and balance your 'bodies.' And remember that as you visit each site, you become a Living Walking Temple carrying the vibrations of that vortex**. It is time NOW**:

*To reconnect with these gateways and vortexes and the power points of these sites and

*To integrate the consciousness of both Lemuria and Atlantis in order for the return to Balance and Peace on Earth. For, as we do this within each one of us, so it manifests in our World.

(Please refer to the Appendix for more details on the Lemurian Energy Sacred Geometry and Affirmations Cards for these Gateways/Temples).

****

Visiting Protocol

The vibrant energies of the temples have been dormant, unplugged, unused for millennia and they are waiting to be re-energized and re-vitalized.

Our mission today is to establish a communication link with these sacred places in order to reboot, revive, reactivate and reawaken their dormant energies. How?

Simply, by visiting these sites, acknowledging the temple's power points and connecting and tuning into their Energies, their Spirit Guides and their Nature Spirits in silence. The temples will respond by establishing a communication link with us. After being re-energized, the temples will light up and will activate the power-filled vibratory grid that surrounds the Earth. They will beckon people to visit them for spiritual and psychic illumination.

The Protocol to follow while visiting these sites:

　　*Ask the Spirit Guardians of the site permission to visit.

　　*Honor them for protecting the site.

　　*Purify yourself from fixed beliefs and past conditionings.

　　*Approach with respect, reverence, honor and integrity.

　　*Connect with the cosmic energies &feel their vibrations.

　　*Have some moments of silence and meditation.

　　*Request your Highest Self to energize you as much as your body can absorb at the time.

　　*Be open and ready to accept and to receive.

　　*Leave a token at the site – a prayer, a song, a flower or a drop of water...in gratitude.

You will then be ready to enter the sacred sites in order to vibrate with the temple's energy fields, to rebalance and reinvigorate your own frequencies, and to hold in your body the powerful energies of the temples in accordance and agreement with your Highest Self. The temples will reawaken our dormant DNA and help our bodies in the process of changing from carbon to crystalline, and be energized with the new vibrational energies of the New Consciousness. In so doing we will energize and heal our planet and restore spiritual and ecological balance to Earth.

Visiting Sacred Sites:

*   ***Activates** Cellular Memories.
*   ***Enhances** Soul Memories and Universal Wisdom.
*   ***Transforms** energy into Light.
*   ***Activates** Physical & Intuitive Abilities.
*   ***Treats** emotional, mental & physical problems.
*   ***Accelerates** personal, group & global evolution.
*   ***Transforms** personal, group & global Karma.
*   ***Regenerates**, recreates and revitalizes our DNA
*   ***Connects** with other sites and people around the globe through the energy grids & vortexes.
*   ***Enhances** the Universal Law of connection linking others who visit. (*Thank you to an anonymous contributor for these reminders*).

"We are destined to be the 'living temples' in the New Era. As the new 'walking temples,' our mission is to bring Light to the world, to be of service and to consciously be

part of the process of creation, to be an example of Light and Peace, and then to share and radiate these wonderful energies consciously. Visiting these sites is surely a highly mystic event and a rewarding experience."

© Francis Xavier Aloisio

****

<u>General Invocation for all the Sacred Sites</u>*:*

I am the Temple of the Light.
I carry the Light of the Sacred Temples within my Heart.
I shine forth the Light from my Heart to the World
So that all may be Temples of the Light!
I am the Temple of the Light. Amen!

****

Recommended Meditation before Visiting the Sites
It is a good idea to clear your vibrational field before moving into these energy vortexes so you may receive them in your bodies in a most gentle and affective way.

The following is a short meditation that will clear your inner being and also ground you, so you may move forward and then vibrate with the energies of the sacred site.

First, it is recommended that you find the **four directions** of where you are standing. With toning a chant or a song, you may face each direction (starting in the East) and honor each one. You may even bow and give thanks in each direction. Then:

*Start releasing by facing West, and standing with feet apart feel the Earth beneath you.

*Envision your feet with roots coming out the bottom of your soles and follow them to the crystal core of Mother Earth.

*Take three breaths slowly into your belly and breathe out, each time the roots grow deeper.

*After you have connected to the crystal core, then bring up your arms again while breathing in.

*As you bring your arms down with hands facing downward, chant: "OM," and when your arms and hands reach your heart center, and "NA" and keep releasing your breath as you come down to the Earth. Repeat 3 times, breathing up from the Earth and then chant as you move your arms over your body.

*Envision white light from the Creator Source coming down through your body and chakras clearing any blocks that you are ready to release as you breathe out and thank Mother Earth for taking them and transmuting them.

*Facing East, bring in the New Energy into your bodies and chakras while taking three slow breaths. (Breathing in with arms outstretched and then breathe out blowing into your heart with your arms and hands.)

*Envision white sparkling rainbows coming into your heart from the East and then moving up and down all your chakras.

Now repeat these movements, vision and breath in all the directions. Finish with a bow to all the directions and end with hands in prayer position over the heart. 'Namaste.'

Suggestions for your Spiritual Journey

*This Handbook offers a Guide to the locality of the sites, and gives a Metaphysical Perspective.

*Each temple has its own colored vortex of energy that vibrates in a Sacred Geometrical Frequency.

*It is important to read the Protocol and do the recommended Meditation before visiting.

*Please note: All the guidance and insights of *Adama* are in **"quotes."**

* Use this guidebook for your own spiritual connection with each temple.

****

The Lemurian Energy Sites
The Specific Purpose and Vibration of each Temple.

THE TEMPLE OF INNER KNOWING - Cambria
Near the very end of Nottingham Street/Pocket Park.

As you enter the park, start moving inside yourself, and at the same time, be aware of the flora and fauna. Reaching the cliff, look down to see a collection of rocks that form somewhat of a circle of dark stones with the waves crashing around them, seen better at low tide.

Adama: "Now look in the center of these stones - it is the vortex of the energy of this Temple. Meditate on these stones, as they hold the vibration of Inner Knowingness. As you become one with them, they will pulsate even more to your willingness to be open to their light. Their light rotates outward and merges into the next Gateway/Temple located off shore at Moonstone Beach, The Bridge Temple.

This Inner Knowing site has the energies of 'True Knowing, Deep Understanding and Open Acceptance.' Here you come in contact with your 'True Self,' the Supreme Inner Knowing.

In this way you get to the center of your 'Core Being.' And it is here that you hold this vibration. It is your Heart Center.

Before and after going to this Temple, practice going into your Heart Center, so when you are in its vibration, you are in a deeper, truer connection to Yourself, the One that is your God-Self.

Come to this Gateway, this Temple, and reach inside and become aware of your Truth. This is the essence of your being. Once you start here, all other situations, places, relationships come to a higher level of understanding."

****

THE BRIDGE TEMPLE - Moonstone Beach, Cambria

You may reach this site by going through Shamel Park or standing above it at Santa Rosa Creek Parking lot.

The circle of stones is a very powerful, prominent configuration, standing close to shore.

Adama: "Situated between two powerful points, this is the gateway or the Bridge that brings Self/Inner Knowing together with the Divine Union of the Inner Masculine and Feminine.

Viewing the vortex of this Temple from shore, it holds the power of your Sacred Heart. The configuration of the stones also pulsates to the Heart of the Universe.

It is the Key to the understanding of Oneself and the Bridge to Your Own Sacred Heart."

****

THE TEMPLE OF DIVINE UNION - North Coast of Cambria

Situated across from San Simeon Lodge and a local restaurant and north of Leffingwell Landing.

Adama: "This temple brings together the Heart and the Mind; the Divine Masculine and the Divine Feminine. These energies flow in the figure 8 symbol, as it moves and flows and constantly balances these two vibrations on our Mother Earth. She is both Masculine and Feminine. She is ALL to us who live within her and on her surface. As above, so below.

One also needs to know one's true self before they can bring this Divine Union into one's being- the balance of the Divine Masculine (the Mind) and the Divine Feminine (the Heart). To know oneself and come to terms with one's being is the first step to bring together, in Divine Union, these two vibrations. The energies of both vibrations are then balanced within.

This temple carries the alignment of the Heart and the Mind: The Feminine with the Masculine. The figure 8 of the

33

sacred geometry of this site symbolizes the continuous flow between these two vibrations.

Know Yourself and bring Divine Union into your own Being. ALL is in Balance. Feel the balance within you!"

****

THE TEMPLE OF HEALING - San Simeon Point - The Cove.

You may walk the beach to the end and connect to the Vortex's vibration in the stones, or walk the trail to San Simeon Point, where you can connect with the stones on the bluff. This is a very large, expansive temple.

Adama: "The Temple of Healing is a very special sacred place. As you know, many people can feel its healing vibrations when they visit without comprehending it. Those who are conscious will receive even more healing as they understand and become aware of this most sacred place. The healing here can be profound if the participant is ready. It will be gentle and nurturing for all those who visit.

During the late Lemurian times, it was used mainly to bring us to a grounding place. We were confused and hurting and having difficulty with our bodies assimilating the new vibrations, as our own world and all we knew was collapsing around us. We came here and received the blessings of the balanced Matrix. The Ley-lines or Electromagnetic energies that stretch between our Healing Temple and the land

34

around your San Miguel Mission, carries with it the matching Matrix.

The Mission was built on a vortex of these Ley-lines and named it for the protection of the Sacred and Secret Illumination that emanates from it. The Natives intuitively knew that energy and so resided there. Then the Christians came and claimed it for their own. Saint Michael and his pure energies, to this day, are a protecting force for not only that place, but of those Ley-lines that lead all the way to the coast and your 'Cove' in San Simeon.

And many would say that the coastline has changed since the Lemurian Era. Yes, it may have changed geologically, but please remember this: that energy is energy and all the stones, cliffs and the sea still vibrate with this same frequency today. It is still there; it is still pure; it is still sacred.

So those who want to begin their journey of connection and raising their vibration, may want to start here at the Temple of Healing, to clear, to balance and to make whole once again their beings on all levels.

Then they will go on to the other temples to integrate this vibration in their bodies, and also to assimilate the new vibrations of each energy point. If you so choose, you may return here after the pilgrimage you made to all the sites, and purify yourself once again for the powerful 'new integration.'

Remember that each individual will respond according to their level of awareness, and what needs to be transmuted for their own highest good, will do so.

This is a Healing Site. Its vibrations are very powerful, yet gentle and nurturing. Feel the shift of your DNA as you enter. It is 'Grounding Place', where you come to 'Clear and Balance' all your energies, where you become 'Whole Again' on all your levels."

****

THE TEMPLE OF WISDOM - Piedras Blancas
Located near the Elephant Seals look-out.

Adama: "As you move through each of these energy fields you will notice a method to which they are introduced. All of these places connect with you and can join with your own vibrations to help you understand your whole being.

Your entire being is shifting into higher and higher vibrations in Divine Order. You will feel these shifts and process what is out of 'sync' or balance within you. These places of energy or points of accessing your higher vibrations, serve you in many different ways. Be as conscious as you can, when coming into these electromagnetic points, to clear and then balance your bodies. As you shift even more into your ascended bodies, you gain a higher Wisdom. This insight activates what is already within you.

36

Now, visiting the energetic point that is called 'The Temple of Wisdom,' know that you are coming back to the understanding of the Heart. You bring all that you are into this vortex and you become at one with your 'Wise Highest Self.'

This sacred place accelerates all that you have gone through into a greater understanding of who you truly are! This is the site of 'Oneness'. It is where you become 'at One with the Wise Higher Self.'

Its energies help you to come back to the greatest understanding of the Heart of the Higher Self, and to gain its Highest Wisdom.

This Higher Consciousness activates what is already within you. Wisdom is knowing 'Who You Truly Are!' And *You* are NOW That!"

****

THE TEMPLE OF VENUS-The Goddess of Love.

Approximately 2 miles North of Piedras Blancas, on Highway 1 through the parking lot and gate; walk the trail onto the beach, or view the 'Venus Rock' from the bluff.

A Message from Queen Venus: "My Dear Sisters and Brothers of Divine Light: Thank you for honoring this balanced place.

I say balanced because the feminine energy here is always centered. The vibrations one feels here are

37

beautifully aligned with the male energies. Even though the Feminine is always prominent in this place, The Masculine resides here as well.

The energy vortex vibrates in such a way that no matter who visits, their inner Divine Masculine and Divine Feminine are always being centered.

You will notice me in a reclining position in a place of rest. This is only part of who I am. I am Venus the Goddess of Love. Yet Love is not always resting and complacent. Love is also action and movement. Like my counterpart, Kali, I can also 'raise the roof' and move this loving energy through you in a most masculine 'way'. Always know however, this is done with a 'Feminine Touch;' the touch that brings into alignment the positive and negative energies within.

I am forceful, yet I am a 'Loving Force.' Be of this knowing as you visit this 'energy point' as I bless each one who enters this balanced, loving and powerful vibration!" *Queen Venus*

****

Adama: "This is where the Feminine energy resides and is aligned with the Masculine. It is a loving, nurturing 'force' that balances all the positive and negative, yin/yang energies within. Feel the Power of this Love and the Wisdom is yours!"

****

THE TEMPLE OF PEACE - South Big Sur

A beautiful bay with large stones in a circle viewed from along Highway One, facing South.

Adama: "Once you have experienced your true Inner Healing, finding and connecting to your Inner-Self, and aligning the Masculine and Feminine energies into a pure Divine Union, you come into the Wisdom of your true self with each of the previous temples.

Now, at this temple of Peace, your true, pure, inner peace is magnified into your whole Being and you carry the Great Peace of the Creator Source within you. This, in turn, mirrors to others and to a world that most readily will accept it, for it is True Peace."

****

So, you have moved through your centering and grounding at the Gateway of Healing; found your true loving self at the Temple of Inner Knowing; connected your mind and heart at the temple of Divine Union, and came to a wise higher state at the temple of Wisdom. You then arrive at the place of the Great Peace of the Creator, which embodies the three energies of Peace: Power, Wisdom and Love. All these energies are now magnified within you and you are ready for the next step on your Lemurian Spiritual Journey!

****

THE TEMPLE OF SUCCESS & PROSPERITY - Pacific Valley- Big Sur

Past Sand Dollar Beach to the left and across from the Park Ranger Station. Notice the ring of stones near the top of the trail. They are all tall, and one in particular, points to the heavens, receiving the energy. Take care of the sagebrush and the seasonal ticks that are protecting this site.

Adama: "As you visit this temple, you are now at another level of the great initiation. The temple of Abundance, Success and Prosperity is special as it mirrors the truth of who and 'how' you are, and *You* are 'Divine Abundance.'

Drink in the Presence of this energy of Prosperity for it is your divine birthright. See all things as being Abundant and more Abundance will flow to you.

Understand this is not 'receivership,' this is getting connected to your Divine Will, Sacred Power and the Absolute Truth of who you are. You are all things, and you are already abundant and prosperous in all things. It is who you are! Reconnect with this energy. It is all around you. It Is You! Drink it in! This temple mirrors the truth about oneself-The Divine Abundance within. Reconnect with this energy, for Abundance is YOUR Divine Birthright!"

****

<u>THE TEMPLE OF ILLUMINATION</u> - Cayucos Beach
Under the water of the bay between the Cayucos Pier and Morro Rock.

Adama: "Know that this temple brings 'light' into 'form.' This light is the Illumination of the Soul - the emanation of the heart! As one is attracted to this light of this temple, one feels the energy of the Illumination of the entire Universe. This light illumines the heart to the point of sprouting its rays into the mind. The sacred mind is of the Earth as well. So the light penetrates the mind of those who enter and also to the Earth, to reactivate the vibrations that lay dormant in her as well as the human mind. As all is one, this vibration of light fills every crevice of the Earth and the mind of humanity. Sit in the vibration and feel the reflection of these rays in the heart as they illumine your mind.

This is the Temple of Illumination, sprouting its rays into your Soul, Mind and Heart. It has the energies of Expansion, Enlightenment and Illumination of the Entire Universe. As your Soul, Mind and Heart are illuminated here, so is Mother Earth."

41

Now that you have made your journey
through all these special energetic sites,
you are endowed with the knowledge
of the reason for their existence.

You were meant to come and connect with each one,
as they have given you the message of Truth.
This truth is the reality of who you are,
beyond all doubt.

They are not only a reminder, but
they instill in you the Power of this Truth.
This is Your Truth: That you are
Holy and Sacred, Wise, Powerful and Loved.

These Lemurian Temples vibrate to the octave
of joining your Soul with your
Physical, Mental, Emotional and Spiritual bodies.
Thank you for taking this important
journey to your "True Self."

****

FURTHER INSIGHTS
from
ADAMA, HIGH PRIEST OF TELOS
about the Lemurian Energies.

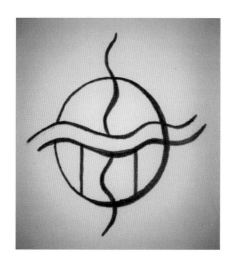

Insights from Adama, the High Priest of Telos, about the energies located under California.

Adama Speaks:

"**Dear Ones, All energy is the same whether you feel it, think it, see it or hear it. ALL energy is the same. So feel the vibrations as you may; the rest will come to you as you get used to this medium. I am here to guide you on this journey. It will be a fun 'ride.'**

Now feel these energies that exist around you and that is what you must go with. Feel in your heart...like the expansion you are feeling now. We are joining our energies and therefore are as one, just as you are one with the ocean, trees and other beings on this wondrous planet.

So, when you feel this energy around you, you are then influenced by vibrations, and become aware of the information that will come to your heart. Your heart is the hearing center for so many of you especially as you are opening up this amazing place within your bodies. Listen to it and let it tell you all you need to know.

The feeling you get from the Atlantean Energies is to heal that part of you that was influenced by your last lifetimes there. Just working to clear this will heal a great many people. The temples in Atlantis (Malta especially) are just as wonderful and energetic as ours were in Lemuria. As you learn more about them, you will find that we were going for the same goal. We wanted the same things and we were in the same energy, for we were one as you and I are.

We are now coming into a time of great healing. Many are going beyond this healing and moving into the light. And it is true that the energies coming in at this moment are shifting us exponentially. This balancing will bring the energies of Atlantis (the Mind) and Lemuria (the Heart) closer together.

Notice the wonderful technology coming forth at this time. So many are now utilizing many of the devices available now. Many more are using these tools for the balancing of these two forces. It is true that we are bringing the best of both worlds together now in this time of plenty.

I did say 'plenty?' Many are feeling the economic pangs of this era. But know this: that you are truly in a time of plenty. Feel the abundance and love that are coming out of these vibrations. They are the balancing force of this shift. Feel these frequencies and offer others to do the same. The best way to influence others is to be in their midst and emanate the love and prosperity you feel. That is the energy of the highest priority. Love, trust, faith and grace are the vibrations that shift us into the next phase.

To do this all you have to do is be! Listen to your heart song. Listen to the vibration of love and joy all around you. Follow the vibration of spirit and know that it is the truth of the Divine Source of all that is. Love and joy and welcome to my world! ***Your Brother, Adama***."

To continue....

"**And so the phase that we have come to right now is an intense stepping up of energies on this planet.**

Everyone is feeling the twinges of fear and so many more are clearing those fears in their daily lives. As these emotions are cleared, the energies will get more intense for they come in when the populace is ready to take them on - I say the majority of the populace.

So we will not speak of ascension here. Because that word is now in the old Paradigm...just as the word 'New Age' is now not sufficient to describe what is happening in our world now. These new actual frequencies are shifting, and we and Mother Earth are vibrating at a faster rate than ever before...this means for all humankind on this planet as well as for those at Inner Earth.

During the Lemurian times and Atlantean times, we were vibrating at a very high frequency as well. After the 'fall,' humanity went to sleep into the dark ages. I call it the dark night of the soul.

You are now coming into a time when these two energies will rise again and awaken with the vibrancy rate that is much higher than when we worked in dualistic cultures. Now we come together in a harmonious 'hummm' with all the 'bells and whistles!' *Adama.*"

****

From Adama for Christine:

"My Dear One, Telos came to be because of our familiarity of the region that it is located beneath, Mount Shasta in Northern California.

The Lemurian people have been in contact with the surface dwellers in this area for a little longer than others due to the expansive understanding of this region known as California.

During the time that the area of Mount Shasta and Telos had been discovered, and subsequently consumed with population, those who came there were drawn because they were ready for change. Now, many generations later, the energy is ripe and ready to show itself. The openness of these light-workers to accept the existence of Telos and that of Lemuria and the Lemurian people is testimony to the level of development that these people attained.

It is time now to introduce them to the actual ancient Lemurian Temples and activate and revive these special vortexes. It is imperative that this continues so that the energies of both Lemuria and Atlantis come back into balance. This is such important work, as now the cosmic climate is moving actively and many will feel the effects. Balance during these times is truly the focus of all of us Lemurians as well as Atlanteans.

It is all coming together now. So I am asking that everyone connect with each other during these times of unity consciousness. Great balance is achieved through learning, awareness and staying open to all presented to you.

Please also connect with any ley-lines, other vortexes and energy centers in this beautiful area known as Lemuria/California. Telos has now expanded as the UnderLand of Lemuria, under what is known as California on the surface. Bring those here when they are ready, to help merge and balance the Lemurian and the Atlantean vibrations. Speak to as many as possible about this merging and also inform them of the Atlantean Crystal City under Malta. *Awareness* is key to this Unity Consciousness, for only then is Evolvement possible. ***Adama***."

APPENDIX

Sacred Symbols of the Temples

In 2010, I received insights of the sacred symbols that vibrate to the Lemurian energy sites on the Central Coast of California in Cambria. The following year, I received further information about the symbols of the sacred temples of Malta and Gozo.

Each temple has its own sacred shape, color and tone that vibrates and pulsates in a Sacred Geometrical patterns. These sacred symbols are 5D Light Frequencies and Energy Pathways that will help us raise our state of consciousness to the next dimension.

These symbols will also allow the energy of the Universe to flow through our being to help us move into a new level of alignment. (*As we have already connected to the shape and color of each temple, we are now in the process of attuning to their frequencies as tones to take ourselves even further into these higher vibrations*).

The symbols and frequencies of corresponding colors have been produced into a beautiful set of cards, each with the vibratory hues and affirmation of the particular temple, as well as for the Crystal City of Telos.

If you feel the call to visit the sites found on Malta or Cambria CA, you will experience first-hand the awe-inspiring rock formations, temples and sacred-energies of these ancient and forgotten civilizations.

Those who cannot physically visit these sites, have now the opportunity to tune in and connect with these sacred and powerful energy sites, as well as the Crystal Cities of Telos and Ashua.ra.ta.ra, through the magic of these sacred symbols.

The special colored set of cards (**11 in each**) of the Sacred Symbols of the Temples can be obtained via email and by post and are available now in its second print with a new additional symbol.

(**See website *www.lemuriaenergyjourneys.com*
for further details**)

Suggestions for use.

You can use these cards in many ways:
 • These cards connect you to the essence and vibration of each temple.
 • They can be used physically at each temple and/or privately in your own space.
 • Each card can be chosen from the deck randomly to see what energy is called for at that time.
 • They can be used as a meditation tool to come into a better understanding of your truth.
 • They can be used also as a tool for inner growth and for spiritual evolution.
 • When choosing a card focus on its sacred symbol and attune to the vibration of the color behind it.
 • You may then apply that color to your everyday life. Some suggestions would be wearing clothes/jewelry, eating food and surrounding yourself within the hue.
 • Use the sacred symbols by tracing or redrawing them as they are being used multi-dimensionally.
 • Read the suggested message and use it for the day or the week to move you to a more powerful connection to the Cosmic Energies.
 • Listen to your intuition for any other suggestions for their use.

****

Glossary

Agartha: The realm beneath the surface of the Earth.

Atlantis: The fourth root race. It was a highly advanced civilization covering the Atlantic Ocean, Southern Europe, northern Africa and parts of the Mediterranean and Asia.

Chakras: Subtle spinning vibrational centers/channels in which vital energy moves and flows through.

Consciousness: The energetic field that makes up everything we see around us. It is the greatest mystery of science.

Dimensional Portal: A star gate between dimensions.

Dimensions: Different realms of realities that are on different levels existence. Our world is a physical manifestation in third dimensional reality.

DNA or nucleic acids: The molecular basis of the cellular double-helix structure that is the blueprint of our being. All knowledge is encoded in our DNA.

Electromagnetic: Energy generated by electricity in magnetic fields.

Extra-terrestrials: Star Beings who came to earth from other planets, stars systems and constellations. They are the 'greater family of man.'

Gaia: Mother Earth. She is now awake and conscious and vibrating in 5th Dimension.

Homo sapiens: All living human beings, who later evolved into the *homo sapiens sapiens* - the double thinking human.

Hula: An ancient native Hawaiian dance.

Lemuria: A land of light located on the island of Mu in the Pacific Ocean area, known as the Motherland of modern humanity. The Lemurians were the third root race and said to be the guiding spirits of the Earth.

Ley-lines: Geometric alignments that travel in a line between sacred sites and can be a part of a grid. They are electromagnetic pathways (telluric currents) that transmit and receive the energies present around the globe.

Malta: A small island in the middle of the Mediterranean Sea. It was the center of the vast territory of the Atlantis Empire. Gozo is the smaller sister island in its archipelago.

Pleiades: The star system known as the Seven Sisters with Alcyone as their central star. **Sirius,** connected to Atlantis, is the closest star to our Solar System and the brightest star in the sky. It is home to the 6D Sirians.

Portal: A large and elaborate doorway or gate that one can move through, physically or etherically.

Sentient Beings: Conscious Beings.

Vortex: The center of converging Electromagnetic Ley-lines that acts as a powerful resonant structure, and purifying energy as it moves in a circle.

****

Main Energetic Rays, Chakras and Vortexes of California

California's name may have come from a phrase meaning 'high mountains,' or from the Arabic, *Calif*, which was understood by the Europeans to mean 'leader.' Queen Califa was associated with the mythical Amazonas, who was known to be the Queen of Lemuria.

In California many sacred sites and temples were built or situated on major pathways of highly charged Electromagnetic Energy. These magnetic fields or grids are the DNA delivery engines of our Planet. There are energetic sites all along the state of California. Lemuria made its home here and Telos is a living Fifth Dimensional Crystal City under California, expanding out from Mt. Shasta. San Francisco is one of the five ancient sites of Lemuria.

To help understand better the significance of the area of San Francisco as an ancient site of Lemuria, the following quote from the book: *The Masters and their Retreats* by Mark L. & E. C. Prophet, gives another point of view:

"The Goddess of Purity's (Etheric) Retreat over San Francisco: The Goddess of Purity holds the focus of one of the ancient Temples of Lemuria in the seven hills of the San Francisco area. The intensity of the flame of purity held in this magnificent retreat is beyond what man can realize. It is a focus of the Mother flame of Mu as well as a focus of the ascension flame. San Francisco is one of five ancient focuses of Lemuria that today are the five secret-ray chakras of the state of California. The retreat of Archangel Gabriel and Hope, located etherically above and between Sacramento and Mount Shasta, is extended for the protection of San Francisco through the (etheric) retreat of the Goddess of Purity."

There are **Five Rays** that are located in California. The rays anchored at these points act as light-filled vortexes that bring balance along the coast against cataclysm and for the transition to the Culture of the Golden-Age.

These sites/cities are: San Juan Capistrano, Santa Barbara, San Luis Obispo, Monterey and San Francisco.

The seven main Chakras of California, from the base to the crown, are: **Root Chakra** - San Diego, **Sacral Chakra** - Los Angeles, **Solar Plexus Chakra** - Bakersfield, **Heart Chakra** - Fresno, **Throat Chakra** - Sacramento, **Third Eye Chakra** - Redding, and **Crown Chakra** - Mount Shasta.

(From *The Masters and their Retreats*
by Mark L. & E. C. Prophet).

Please remember that these chakras are spinning ever outwardly to enhance the vibration of the land surrounding them. Being in the area around or between these sites will influence the frequency you are on. You could say they are vortexes, and as with any change of vibration, they can shift and move to other areas.

****

The Missions of California

San Diego was the first mission in a chain of twenty-one missions established by the Spanish on Native American energy sites. It is located on the current Root Chakra of California.

These missions followed the Ley-lines up the state of California through the highly vibrational vortexes that were settled by the local Native tribes. Most of these settlements were originally used by the Lemurians; the Natives intuitively felt this and established their homes there.

Countless Native Americans were massacred by the Spaniards and the Church as their sacred homes and camps were taken away from them. Many more died from the diseases that were contracted from these invaders.

As you follow the Catholic Mission placements of California you will find that they were settled on these highly vibrational vortexes in order to acquire, use and cap their powers. Knowingly or unknowingly, the Christian Era took over these sites to prevent the Sacred Knowledge of Native Americans from spreading and therefore kept much of humanity in the dark for hundreds of years, and even longer.

This wisdom of the Natives has kept the Legacy of the Ancient Lemurians sacred, and these peaceful tribes held this knowledge close to their hearts. The Sacred Knowledge and insights of their ancestors were entrusted to these non-violent people.

The Chumash, Salinian and other tribes that called this land their home were indeed, a very peace-loving people. Unlike some of their brothers and sisters of the rest of America, they kept to themselves and traded with each other, instead of fighting.

These were the true ancestors of the Lemurians and these tribes held a closer link to them. Since they were not warriors, they had no way to defend themselves from the European and religious invaders. Those who did not perish were swallowed up in the religion of their conquerors.

Visiting these missions you may be able to heal these past atrocities by connecting to the original vibration of the Native Americans that lived there.

Some of the areas are still vibrating to the frequency of the vortex that is also part of the Ley-Line/Grid network of Electromagnetic Energy.

Even the placement of the buildings that are situated on the land or found to be decorated inside, you will be able to tell that at some level, these ancient sites are still carrying the beautiful energies of Lemuria.

****

Chumash Nation
The Chumash Natives numbered in the tens of thousands before the Spanish arrived in what is now California. They called themselves the *First People* and the Pacific Ocean was their first home.

The Chumash name means 'Breadmaker' or 'SeaShell People' and their resources were the land and the sea. They kept a perfect balance of Earth and Sea.

Their ceremonies and rituals were held to honor the seasons. During Winter Solstices the Shaman priests led several days of dancing and feasting to honor the power of their father, the Sun. They used caves for sacred religious ceremony where their history was passed down from generation to generation through stories and legends. Interestingly, women could serve equally as chiefs and priests. One priest could be responsible for several villages.

Each Shaman was also an astrologer. The Astronomers of the village would chart the heavens and then the astrologer would interpret and guide the people. They believed that the world was in a constant state of change, so the decisions in the villages were only made after consulting the charts.

Many of their stories as well as their tribe were all but decimated in the 1700's and 1800's by the Spanish Mission system. The Land of the Chumash was given off to the control of the Missions, then eventually in land grants to Spanish families loyal to the Mexican government.

Other tribes along the Central coast were the *Pomo* who were known for their basket weaving as well as the *Miwok* and *Wappo* Tribes. The *Salinian* Tribes who lived in what is now the Big Sur region were known as the Esalens.

****

The map included in this book points out the Lemurian Vortexes/Temples along the Central Coast of California.

As you look inland on the map, notice some of the missions that were built on Native American villages. These were all localized to the Electromagnetic Ley-Lines that connect them to the Temples located on the coast.

One in particular is **San Miguel Mission** sitting on the same Ley-Line as the San Simeon Point Temple of Healing. Interestingly, on the same Ley-Line, and in between these two points, stands Hearst Castle. Mr. Hearst seemed to have honed in on the vibration of this site.

This also seemed to have occurred with **San Antonio Mission** that lies eastward, and on the same Ley-Line as the Temple of Abundance and Prosperity. Not only was a mission built there, but Mr. Hearst also built a mansion not far from it.

Curiously, both the mission of San Antonio and the mansion are surrounded by a US military base!

****

Central Coast of California-Cambria

Etheric Temples of Lemuria and some corresponding *Missions*:

North > South
Abundance/Prosperity >
San Antonio Mission

Peace
Venus
Wisdom

Healing >
San Miguel Mission
Divine Union
The Bridge
Inner knowing
Illumination

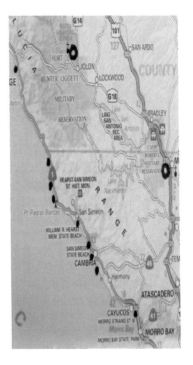

(Map from California Division of Tourism)

The Ten Dimensions & how to relate to them.

It is important at this time of our Cosmic Awakening to understand and remember that we are all multidimensional beings. Below are the dimensions and their descriptions to help us in this process. They will help you to connect to the truth of who you are. When identifying with each dimension we actually become that which we acknowledge. We become our true Multidimensional Self.

* **The 1st Dimension** is the Iron Core Center of the Earth whose purpose is to draw you to itself. **Keeper: The Hexagonal Iron Crystal.** Stand in the center of the 4 directions facing East and acknowledge each one while giving honor and tribute and connecting your core with that of Gaia's.

* **The 2nd Dimension** is the realm between the Core of Gaia and the Earth's crust. We are linked here through chemical, radioactive, mineral and crystalline essences that are also present in our bodies. **Keepers: Elementals.** Connect deep into Mother Earth and call upon the Elementals to come forth for healing and to be part of your being. Honor them for their work.

* **The 3rd Dimension** is composed of all life on the Earth's surface. **Keepers: Human Beings.** Honor the powers of the 1st and 2nd dimensions as well as your own body and surface creatures, water, stone and plants and consciously work with them. Get in touch with yourself and all beings through your heart.

* **The 4th Dimension** is the realm of the human collective of mind, emotions and feelings. **Keepers: Annunaki** (Sumerian Beings from Nibiru). By following your fascinations and stop any judgement you can clear emotions that block you from moving forward.

* **The 5th Dimension** is the realm of Love that expresses the energy of the whole Universe. **Keepers: The Pleiadians.** This

dimension is related to the heart. Keep your heart open as you center yourself there in your feelings and radiate love to yourself and all that surrounds you.

* **The 6th Dimension** is the realm of geometric forms that replicates in 3D. **Keepers: The Sirians**. Connect to the geometrical matrix of your mind to create in 3rd dimension, and as you join your heart (5D) to your mind (6D) you expand your field of potentiality. (Examples: architecture, building, yoga, design…)

* **The 7th Dimension** is the realm of Cosmic Sound - the Galaxy's communication system. **Keeper: Andromeda**. Surround yourself with the beauty of sound that *connects* you with all life. The sounds of the stars, planets as well as singing, music and birds will bring you into a closer relationship with the Galaxy and all of Life.

* **The 8th Dimension** is the realm of the Divine Mind organized by the Galactic Federation. **Keeper: Orion.** As you come in contact with the Divine Mind you can access all other beings contained in our Galaxy and beyond.

* **The 9th Dimension** is the Milky Way itself; a dimension that emanates out of its black hole. Some call this the Great Central Sun. **Keeper: Tzolkin** - the Mayan Spinner of the Time Waves. When coming into Samadhi (connection to all), you become one with all beings of light - Pure light and Pure energy of all Truth.

* **The 10th Dimension** is the vertical axis that generates all Nine Dimensions.

(Adapted from *The Alchemy of the Nine Dimensions* and *The Pleiadian Agenda* by Barbara Hand Clow).

****

Connecting with the Author

Website: www.lemuriaenergyjourneys.com
Onstellar: https://onstellar.com/Auriela
Facebook: http://facebook.com/christine.auriela
Email: christine.aloisio@gmail.com

****

Second Publication: *The Crystal City of Atlantis* – My Journey to Ashua.ra.ta.ra. "This timely and momentous book launches us into the discovery of an Atlantean Crystal City under the Island of Malta. It also follows the spiritual journey of the author through her life experiences and how she found a very special valley on that unique island."

Both books are available as *PDF* from the author (email).

****

To connect with the Prehistoric Temples of Malta
visit website: www.maltatemplejourneys.com

****

Francis Xavier Aloisio published the novels: *Islands of Dream, The Age of Magic and Wisdom, The New Temple Dreamers, The Islands of Dream Speak* and the guidebook *An Alternative Handbook to the Maltese Temples*. These are available as PDF from the author and also from Smashwords and other online bookshops, and from the main bookshops on Malta as Hardcopies.

****

About the Author

Christine Auriela Aloisio has lived in Cambria on the Central Coast of California for over 25 years. She connects strongly to her Cosmic and Native American descent.

Along with spearheading and hosting many local 'Wellness Fairs,' she is also the past owner of *7 Sisters Mystical Emporium* in Cambria, California. This center held classes and ceremonies for spirituality and self-awareness for all beliefs and paths, as well as books and products.

Through her current travels to many energy sites in Hawaii, French Polynesia, England, Finland, Sweden, Austria and Malta, Christine is now paving the way for others to reconnect with their Atlantean and Lemurian heritage. Her purpose is to help bring the best of both worlds back into alignment and balance as we recreate the New Golden Age - the 'Era of Remembering.'

Christine and her husband, Francis, are authors and facilitators to the Maltese Temples and the Energy sites of California.

This handbook was written to be a *personal guide* to those who are called to visit these etheric sacred sites.

Joyful 'journeying!'

The Coming Together and the Balance of the
Masculine and Feminine Energies
(The Sword and the Cup)
Located at the Temple of Success and Prosperity
Big Sur – California.

****